Driving Test Confidence

Maria McCarthy

Driving
Test
Confidence

Helpful and inspiring tips to guide you from your very first lesson to driving test success

First published in 2024
Copyright © Maria McCarthy 2024 – first edition

The moral rights of the author have been asserted.

ISBN paperback – 978-1-7384529-2-7
ISBN ebook – 978-1-7384529-3-4

A catalogue record for this book is available from the British Library.

IMPORTANT NOTE TO READERS
This book has been written and published for informational and educational purposes only.
Any use of information in this book is at the readers' discretion and risk. The author cannot be held responsible for any loss, claim or damage arising out of the use or misuse of the suggestions made. No liability is assumed by the author the reader is entirely responsible for his or her own actions.

ABOUT THE AUTHOR
Maria McCarthy is a motoring journalist writing for national magazines and newspapers. She broadcasts on motoring matters and has appeared on BBC Breakfast, Sky, ITN and carried out over 2000 radio interviews. She is also the author of *Driving Test Secrets You Need to Know, 50 Ways to Overcome Driving Test Nerves* and *You can Pass Your Driving Test*.

Book cover and interior design – Design for Writers

Contents

A NOTE FROM THE AUTHOR

CHAPTER 1

CONFIDENCE IS KEY

Welcome to *Driving Test Confidence,* which is part of my *Driving Test Confidence* series of books, designed to help you learn to drive and pass your test in a way that's as safe and stress-free as possible.

When it comes to passing your driving test, using tailored strategies for building your confidence will really help you. Some people pick up driving skills very quickly and take that sense of ease and competence into the test situation. Others find the whole process challenging, from their very first lesson to the stomach-churning anxiety of test day. Most of us are somewhere in between, though mostly clustered up the stressful and stomach-churning end. For the record, I'm a motoring journalist who has been published in national newspapers and magazines and I failed my first driving test through nerves – thankfully I passed on my second attempt!

Whatever your natural aptitude, developing greater confidence can help you. By that of course I don't mean unrealistic confidence. There are a lot of situations where 'fake it till you make it' can get you through, but learning to drive isn't one of them. No matter how much you ramp up your self-belief, you're still going to have to get to grips with the practical techniques of driving and road craft and make your peace with the fact that this can be a lengthy and expensive process. Diligently repeating affirmations along the lines of 'I am a brilliant driver' when you're still messing up most of your reverse parks and terrified of overtaking isn't going to cut it.

What is truly transformative is developing the sort of grounded, realistic confidence that respects where you are currently are on your learning to drive journey whilst also knowing you are capable of getting better, going further, passing your test and becoming a safe driver for life.

Most advice about driving test confidence focuses on boosts you can give yourself in the few hours before your test. They include practising calming breathing techniques, knocking back Bach Rescue Remedy and of course the ever-popular 'eat a banana'. I'm a great fan of all of these, and cover the whys and wherefores of how they can help in this book and others. But to reap the real benefits of inner confidence it's important to start at the very beginning. Before you even sit in the driving seat of a car you can lay the groundwork by finding the right instructor, developing a workable budget to fund your lessons and getting to grips with the Highway Code and rules of the road. Once your lessons begin it's massively helpful to have the confidence to communicate honestly with your instructor.

Then there's the form of confidence that helps you avoid 'comparison-itis' – measuring the lessons and tests you need against those of your friends or siblings and feeling miserable and inadequate as a result. We all learn different skills at different paces, and comparison-itis is hugely unhelpful, so refusing to join with that particular downward spiral can only be a good thing. And then of course there's maintaining a positive and focused attitude on driving test day. Responsible driving instructors don't put their pupils forwards for their test until they're sure they're ready to pass, so the only thing that can scupper you at this point are the dreaded driving test nerves. *Driving Test Confidence* contains lots of techniques for helping you overcome them, so you're certain to find some that resonate with you.

This book and my others offer lots of practical advice, reassuring support and a range of proven tips and techniques to help make both learning to drive and passing your test easier and less stressful. They also include useful, relatable and often very funny stories from driving instructors and other learner drivers. With my best wishes for your successful test pass and a future of safe and happy driving.

Maria xxx

1. Listen to advice from instructors

Don't think that being a bag of nerves before your test means you're going to fail. I've seen learners who are visibly trembling as they walk over to greet their examiner return to me with a big grin on their face, brandishing their test pass certificate. It can feel very tense in the waiting room, but once the test begins and candidates have something to concentrate on, most find that their anxiety decreases and they are able to drive well. *Aaron 31, driving instructor*

When we're in the waiting room I say to my learners, 'I don't put anyone forward for their test unless I feel sure they have what it takes to be a safe, capable driver. I believe you deserve to be here and to pass your test. All you have to do is believe it too'. *Danielle 56, driving instructor*

If you're an older driver or struggling with confidence or co-ordination issues, you might like to consider learning in an automatic. For some people combining 'car craft' – that is, operating the gears and clutch with 'road craft', which is navigating traffic and road conditions is overwhelming for them. Automatics are easier to drive as there's less 'car craft, involved. Some learners start on an auto straight away, whilst others may have tried manual cars first. In the latter case, by the time they get to me their self-esteem when it comes to driving can be very low and I have to work with them on building that up, alongside their practical skills. It's very satisfying for me as an instructor to watch pupils who may have struggled previously make better progress just by switching to a simpler automatic car. And of course electric vehicles (EVs) don't have gears so if you only plan to run and drive EVs then you would only need an automatic licence. *Mark 46, driving instructor*

All examiners have to have similar pass rate to that of their colleagues at the test centre, so it doesn't make any difference whether your examiner is the friendly type or more reserved – you have the same chance of passing, whoever you get. You can chat to them during the test if it helps put you at ease, but if you'd rather not just let them know. They want you to be as relaxed as possible so you can drive confidently and safely. *Emily 28, driving instructor*

2. Listen to advice from successful learners

Stay focused on your driving and don't worry about mistakes that you may or may not have made earlier in your test. Put them behind you and move on. I passed my test on the second attempt after what I believed to be an automatic fail within about two minutes of leaving the test centre. I had to do an emergency stop when a cyclist appeared from no-where and rode directly in front of me. He yelled and shook his fist at me as if I was in the wrong. I resigned myself to failure and decided I would relax and at least keep my number of faults to a minimum. But at the end of the test my examiner said that I'd handled the situation with the cyclist very well and that I was now a licensed driver. *Jacob, 42*

Don't tell anyone the date of your test. At first I told my family and friends and got loads of messages of support which was lovely. But then when I failed (and kept on failing) it created even more pressure as I had to deal with other people's disappointment as well as my own. After my second failed test I didn't tell anyone outside of my immediate family – and it made it even more fun when I was able to message everyone a picture of myself holding my test pass certificate and get so many congratulations! *Kira, 19*

The most important thing is to find the right instructor – make contact and chat with a few to find one you feel you'll be happy to spend a few hours a week with, guiding you through both the good times and the bad. And don't just choose on price. Experienced instructors might cost more but if you're with an instructor who's the right fit for you then you'll learn more easily and need fewer lessons so it'll work out cheaper overall. My instructor Ravi had done lots of additional courses in counselling and teaching skills, and I always felt he was committed to getting the best out of me. *Maura, 25*

Get in as much practice as you can and with different people if possible. I was lucky that my mum, dad and grandad were all willing to take me out. *Fergus, 20*

Take some exercise before your test if possible. My driving test was in the afternoon and I was worried that I'd get more and more anxious as the day went on, so I went for a swim at lunchtime, as that always helps calm me down. *Dan, 18*

You're not too old and it's not too late. At **48** I was a very reluctant learner and there were times I thought I'd never make it, but with a supportive instructor and a lot of determination and patience I finally got my driving licence. *Joanne, 48*

3. Hang on to your sense of humour

When you're in the thick of your learning to drive journey, wrestling with feelings of inadequacy over your reverse parking skills, worrying about your impending driving test and gripped by abject terror about how much money is being haemorrhaged from your (or your parents') bank account, it can be difficult to keep a sense of perspective. But one day you'll have that coveted driving licence and the whole process will be one you can view through the rear-view mirror - and hopefully remember some funny things that happened along the way!

I started learning to drive at 17 and would go out practising with my dad. One day we were driving over a very narrow hump-backed bridge. Looking back I'm still not not completely sure how I managed it, but somehow I must have got the car at an angle because it got jammed on the bridge. I couldn't move it forwards, and I couldn't reverse back, no matter how much I tried. My dad couldn't work out what to do either and was getting flustered. Queues of traffic started to build up on both sides, and I could see some people were laughing, whilst others were getting impatient and tooting their horns. It was more than I could cope with. So impulsively I just got out of the car, and walked off, leaving my dad to sort it all out. I regretted it before I was five minutes down the road, but by then it felt too late to turn round and go back. When my dad got home he was properly annoyed with me and I felt very ashamed of myself. But now over 20 years later the 'Do you remember when Lauren got the car stuck on a hump-backed bridge and then just walked off?' story has turned into one of those family legends and we can both (genuinely) laugh about it. *Lauren, 39*

It took me eight attempts to pass my driving test. I became a very familiar face to the reception staff at the driving test centre and most of the examiners. I used to say that they'd have to invite me to their Christmas party. *Sian, 26*

My aunt learned to drive back in the 1980s . She always tells this story about how on her first test she was so nervous she accidentally put her front door key into the car lock. It jammed, she couldn't get it out again and the test had to be cancelled. She passed on her fifth attempt. I've been in her car as a passenger and although she's not the best driver I've ever been out with, she's a long way off being the worst! *Jack, 18*

My mate ate some dodgy food and turned up to his driving test the next day with an upset stomach. He told me that about ten minutes in he broke wind and it smelt really bad. The examiner didn't say anything, just quietly wound the window down. He did pass his test though, and I joked that it was only because the examiner didn't want to risk getting stuck in a car with him again! *Ali, 18*

4. 'Let it all be easy' visualisation

Visualisation is where you imagine a particular scenario, and by doing so you 'rehearse' and become more comfortable with it in your mind, and hence are more likely to be able to make it come true in the real world. When applied to learning to drive and passing your test, it's about keeping your focus more on positive, successful outcomes than negative ones. Some people might see visualisation as a bit 'woo-woo' but the fact is we do it all the time. Worrying, for example, basically involves looking at a particular situation and thinking of the ways it could either go wrong or get worse. Worrying is considered perfectly normal and a lot of people spend huge chunks of their life doing it. Visualisation is similar, but the difference is that it involves looking at ways a particular situation could go well or get better. Your imagination is a powerful tool and you can use visualisation to focus your mind on the direction you want your life to go.

One of the stumbling blocks people can encounter when they engage in visualisations is a problem with imagining things and experiences they haven't actually had. Children don't have any difficulty with that, and can effortlessly daydream about being a pirate, a vet or a professional ballet dancer. But as we get older we tend to block our imaginations by telling ourselves that we've got to 'stay realistic'.

When it comes to improving your driving, it's possible to 'stay realistic' and engage the power of visualisation at the same time. You can do this by focusing on an experience that is already real, and then expanding on it. This process can be done in stages, so it always feels grounded and achievable.

What you need to do is to wait until you have learned a few driving skills that you have come to find 'easy'. On your very first lesson your instructor will have taught you the basics of pulling into and away from the kerb, and over time you'll have learned to trundle fairly capably around suburban streets. If you're lucky enough to be able to do private practice with family and friends, you might have carried out simple drives such as supermarket trips, which involve a short distance and often ample parking. These experiences represent 'easy driving'. You can do them and they're not stressful.

However, as lessons progress, instructors often focus more on the skills you find challenging as they want to help you make progress with them. That's an efficient use of your lesson time but it can leave you feeling that driving is always difficult and challenging and completely bypass the fact that it can also be straightforward and fun.

The way to get past this is to ask your instructor to let you do some 'easy driving'. Explain to them that you'd appreciate a brief break from focusing on any 'problem areas' and that spending some time driving at a level where you can feel capable and need minimal guidance will give your confidence a much-needed boost. Hopefully your instructor will understand and tailor a lesson, or part of a lesson to your request.

You then have a memory, or memories to work with that involve 'easy driving'.

Then when you are at home or anywhere else you feel comfortable, you can do your 'Driving is Easy' visualisation. This can work best when you use the 'ladder technique', progressing one or two steps up from where you currently are, rather than going from bumbling, hesitant learner to super-confident race-track type.

Alternatively, if you'd rather plunge straight into a visualisation of yourself as a licensed driver tackling hairpin bends as you drive through the Alps in a sports car, then crack on – it's your visualisation!

Here's an example of how the 'ladder technique' approach might work:

You're driving through suburban streets with a low speed limit. You're comfortable with this, tootling along, keeping an eye out for other road users, maybe chatting with your instructor and generally feeling calm and confident.

Now breathe deeply, allowing yourself to really own and integrate that calm, confident feeling. See it not as a fleeting experience, but as something that's rock solid. As a driver you will always have it. Whatever road or traffic conditions might throw at you, you'll feel at ease, because you know you're skilled and capable.

Now imagine a different scenario . You've moved onto a busy road and are approaching a roundabout. But you haven't tensed up or become anxious in any way. You're still breathing calmly and steadily. You're not second-guessing what your instructor is thinking you should do, because you've covered this in previous lessons. You know you can handle the roundabout easily, and you do.

Now let the scenario transform into your driving test. Yes, there's someone in a hi-viz jacket in the passenger seat, and occasionally they make notes on their tablet. But that's all fine. And although it's officially a 'test' you know that there's nothing for you to worry about. The days of getting flustered or forgetting what you've been taught are long behind you. Even if you're asked to handle exceptionally busy junctions or tricky hill starts, you still have the same level of calm you felt driving around suburban streets, because you've been taught all the skills you need to be a licensed driver and have integrated them so well that they are completely automatic now. You are alert, but at the same time relaxed. Safe driving comes easily and naturally to you.

When you return to the test centre and your examiner informs you that you've passed you're pleased, but not surprised. It's what you expected.

As well as using visualisation, you can also use the 'driving is easy' technique to build up your confidence during regular lessons. For example if you've just navigated a roundabout correctly (even one with no traffic on it!) say to yourself, 'that was easy' or 'I handled that well'. The experience of even small successes will help you relax and feel more open to both further learning and ultimately driving test success.

> I didn't find that driving skills came naturally to me and it took me four attempts to pass my test. There were times I wondered if I'd ever make it, but one of the things that kept me going was the supermarket runs I did with my husband. I realised I could easily do the drive, find parking, and often top up with fuel at the petrol station without any input from him at all. At that point I was still a long way off test standard, but it was like a seed of a 'real driver' had been planted and I knew that by allowing the time and doing the work, I could grow into 'a real licensed driver'. *Jenny, 37*

5. Pin up a map of your driving test centre area

Some people have a naturally good sense of direction and are also good at 'orientating themselves'. They can wander at ease around a foreign city on holiday, and even if they've walked through a variety of different districts they still have that homing-pigeon instinct when it comes to finding their way back to the railway station or hotel. I personally am not one of those people, and if you're not one either, you might find pinning up a map of your test centre area and marking the routes on it helpful. It is of course important to mention that driving test routes are by no means set in stone. The centres often change them, and they can also be altered because of roadworks and diversions. Also, I'm aware that physical print maps are very old-school, but they are still available, and it can be surprisingly useful to have a map up on your wall, rather than poring over one on your phone. It can help you see how the different areas of your city fit together and this can make you feel more grounded and in control.

I live in the St Thomas part of Exeter. I know it well, and also the city centre and nearby areas such as Exwick. But when I was learning to drive I realised that there were parts of the city I'd never visited, such as business parks and suburbs on the edge where I didn't have any friends or reason to go. I found putting up a map and also cycling around the city made me a more confident driver. There were some mini-roundabouts in the Pinhoe suburb I'd found tricky to handle and as we were driving through the streets approaching them on my second driving test I was able to mentally prepare myself. *Kris, 21*

6. Play with a toy car

Learning to drive doesn't always have to be serious – and sometimes quirky techniques such as playing with a toy car can be surprisingly useful. You can also see your toy car as a good-luck mascot, and a forerunner of the full-sized one you'll have in real life eventually.

I'd failed three driving tests and was becoming increasingly desperate when I came across an article saying that boys learn to drive more easily because they grow up playing with toy cars and trucks and hence feel more comfortable around mechanical things. Shortly afterwards I was in a charity shop and spotted a little red toy car with a sunroof, which I bought. I 'practised' with that car, putting a book on the table and 'reversed it round the corner of the book' and also 'parallel parked' it along one edge, between a couple of paper-clip boxes. I did feel I gained extra insights by looking at the car from above, and seeing how it swung into position. I kept the car on my desk and would play with it sometimes. I do feel it gave me a better understanding of manoeuvres. The weirdest thing was after I finally passed test number four and I was looking for a car, a neighbour said he had one to sell. It was a good-value reliable family car – which just so happened to be red with a sunroof! *Jenny, 37*

CHAPTER 2

GETTING INTO GEAR

1. Stay hydrated

When you're stressed your body produces cortisol. Cortisol creates symptoms such as a racing heart, shortened breath and sweaty palms. Staying hydrated dilutes the cortisol in your body and helps you feel calmer. Ideally drink pure water rather than tea or coffee, and definitely avoid energy drinks before a driving lesson or test – you want to avoid feeling jangled or hyped-up. It's best to drink in small sips, so that your body can properly absorb the water rather than glugging it back, which, apart from anything else, is likely to make you need the loo at inconvenient times.

And while we're on the subject of bodily functions, don't feel awkward if you need the loo during a driving lesson. Your instructor will be used to this, so just let them know. Usually they'll just direct you on a route which has a convenient public toilet and you can use that. When it comes to your driving test, bear in mind that not all driving test centres have toilets. Ask your instructor what the situation is at your local one, and make sure you have the opportunity to answer any call of nature just before your test – then it's one less thing to worry about!

2. Really nail down the Highway Code and Theory Test

The UK theory test is comprised of two parts – a multiple choice section followed by a hazard perception test. You need to pass the theory test before you can take your practical test. As soon as you start to think about learning to drive I'd suggest you get hold of a copy of The Driver and Vehicle Standards Agency (DVSA) book, *The Official DVSA Theory Test for Car Drivers* and learn the contents inside out, back to front and sideways. It's important reading, whether you're a car driver, cyclist or a pedestrian. In print form it's a weighty tome, containing hundreds of questions which are very similar to the ones you'll be asked on the test. They include sections on topics such as road and traffic signs, safety margins and motorway driving. You also get to learn about vehicle loading, handling incidents, accidents and emergencies, insurance and road tax, among many other things.

Getting a strong grounding in the rules of the road and consolidating that as you learn with your driving instructor is a valuable experience that will benefit you for the rest of your life. The DVSA book and other learning materials very much encourage active learning and reflection, with sections for you to discuss various rules and safety issues with your driving instructor and tips on integrating them into your lessons and driving practice. There are also links to other relevant publications and useful online videos.

Please don't skimp on this important learning opportunity by just cramming for your theory test a few days or a week in advance. Being a good driver involves having the ability to make confident, split-second decisions. If you ever need to hesitate because you're not quite sure what a particular road sign or direction means, that will make you unsafe on the road. Revise thoroughly, and when you're out and about as a pedestrian, passenger or learner driver consolidate that knowledge through looking at traffic signs, road markings and how others observe (or don't, in some cases....) the rules of the road. That will help you develop an inner sense of confidence and competence that will also support your practical driving sessions.

It also means that you'll know exactly what to do on your driving test and that unexpected situations won't phase you.

> I was driving down a fairly quiet road during my first driving test when an elderly lady came out in front of me. She was clearly very confused and wasn't really crossing the road, more wandering around on it. I wasn't sure what to do, so slowed right down until finally she moved on and I could resume a normal speed. But I failed because of an observation fault. Also in that situation I should have followed rule 112 of the Highway Code which states that 'you should use your horn to alert other road users to your presence' in a dangerous situation.
> *Georgia, 33*

3. Get help for any special needs

If you have a physical disability, or have any issues such as autism, it can be helpful to get tuition that is tailored to your needs. Do some online research, talk to family and friends or contact relevant charities who can offer advice and help you contact suitable driving instructors. You should also inform the DVSA when booking your test, as although all drivers have to reach the same standard of skill, some adaptions can be made.

I'm deaf and most of my deaf friends learned on automatic cars. They can be easier for deaf people as you don't have to hear the revs. But I want to work as a builder and might need to drive work vans so I knew I wanted a manual licence. I am good with mechanical things so I reckoned I'd be OK from the practical side, but finding the right instructor took some work. I can lip-read, so I knew my instructor could communicate with me that way, but it meant they'd have to explain things when we were parked up as I wouldn't be able to look at them closely enough to lip-read while we were actually driving. It's also helpful for instructors to use diagrams and sketches when teaching deaf people, and if they know British Sign Language (BSL) then obviously that's even better. Eventually I found an instructor called Gabi who sounded just right. She was interested in helping learners with special needs and had done counselling courses and was learning BSL. Gabi was an excellent instructor. When it came to my driving test, I discovered that deaf people are allocated a longer time for their test. They still do exactly the same amount of driving, but it's to cover the additional time you'll spend preparing with the examiner before setting off and also parked up while they explain the next part of the test. For example, the examiner will show you what gestures they will make to indicate what they would like you to do, whether that's pulling over or making a particular manoeuvre. It's allowed to have your instructor along not just as an observer, but to interpret the examiner's requests if necessary. I had Gabi along, but as it happened I didn't need her as I was able to communicate with my examiner without extra help. I passed first time with only two minors, which was great! *Jack, 18*

4. Can private practice make me more confident?

The answer to this question is mostly yes – but sometimes no. It depends on what sort of private practice you do and, most importantly, who you do it with! I cover the topic of private practice in more depth in another of my books, *You Can Pass Your Driving Test*, outlining the best strategies for making it work effectively and stating the legal requirements. You can also find the latter information online on the website for your government or State. In the UK it is on the gov.uk and readytopass websites

In this chapter I just want to emphasise the key points as related to building and maintaining your confidence at the wheel. I'd encourage you, your supervising driver and your instructor to liaise about what type of practice would be most beneficial. The key rule of thumb is that your supervised drives should always be at a level that's significantly below what you're doing with your driving instructor. Your supervising driver won't have dual controls or be experienced in helping another driver get out of a tricky situation, so safety should always be your key concern. Most learners find that doing easy drives close to home works best initially as often they can be carried out without any input from their supervisor, meaning they begin to feel like 'a real independent driver'.

One important factor to bear in mind however, is the relationship between you and your supervisor while practising. It has the potential to build your confidence or seriously damage it! Even harmonious relationships can feel the strain under the pressure of learning to drive – and ones that are already a bit wobbly can crumble completely. On the plus side, if it works well it can be a fun, bonding experience.

Go into private practice with an open mind – if it works, that's great and if it doesn't then it's best to resign yourself to the fact that you'll have to fork out for more lessons.

Here's some examples of how private practice can work out in families:

> I got really annoyed with my mum when we went out practising as she would not get off her phone, even though she wasn't meant to use it when she was supervising me. She always wanted to send 'just one more text'. *Kris, 21*

When I became a teenager I started hanging out with my mum rather than my dad, because we had more in common. But when I started to learn to drive and was desperate to practise as much as possible, my dad was more willing to come out with me. He was really calm and encouraging. My older brothers can drive but they're not that bothered about cars, whereas I love them and so does my dad. Having this shared interest was great, and brought us closer together. *Sasha, 17*

My dad and I used to practise manoeuvres in the car park at the local cemetery. He'd make the same joke every time. 'No need to worry about injuring anyone here Lauren, they're already dead'. *Lauren, 39*

And some examples of practising with a partner:

I did go out practising with a partner when I was in my late 20s. Jasper was a fellow lawyer and we'd just got engaged. He lived in Clapham and we went for a few joyless trundles around local streets. He used to do this patronising little smirk when I got things wrong (which I did a lot). I started to wonder if in some way he was enjoying watching me flounder, because it made him feel more capable and powerful. Initially I just put it down to a lack of confidence making me paranoid. But then one day I messed up a reverse around a corner and glanced over at Jasper who was sitting there smirking away. And it was clouds had parted and something shifted in me and I thought, 'I'm not in love with you any more and I can't imagine why I ever thought I was in the first place'.

I ended our engagement a couple of days later and I think he was relieved to be free of it as well. The stresses and strains of driver practice had shown us both a side of the other person's character we hadn't really liked – and finding that out before the wedding rather than afterwards saved us both a trip to the divorce courts. *Chloe, 42*

My husband had to surrender his licence after he had his stroke, so having supervised practice with him wasn't an option. But I'm aware that going out practising with a learner-driver spouse can put a lot of strain on a relationship, so at least we didn't have to worry about that! *Jane, 58*

I'd heard stories from my friends about how driving practice sessions with their partners had ended in rows and tears, so I was apprehensive about going out with my husband Matt. But to our surprise it was really good fun. We'd agreed beforehand that we wouldn't do anything stressful, like endless bay parks, or tricky junctions, but instead just have a relaxing drive around the local countryside. My mum looked after our three young children when we were out driving and we discovered it was a fantastic opportunity to reconnect and chat as a couple. It helped that I had a great instructor and enjoyed driving from my very first lesson, so although I had my ups and downs, I wasn't stressed out by the process in the way I know some people are. A typical practice session would involve driving about half an hour, taking a short walk and then returning home, stopping off to do a couple of reverse parks somewhere. As I grew closer to my test, we would sometimes take the children somewhere like the supermarket, so I'd be used to driving with them in the back once I was an independent driver. *Carla, 29*

And friends:

I do have some friends who could potentially have supervised my driving practice, but at my age I'd have felt too embarrassed. As an older learner I was in a position to pay for additional lessons, so I just did. *Jacob, 42*

I bought a car to practise on and a real turning point for me was when a licensed-driver friend came to stay just a few days before my second test and we drove to get a takeaway. She's fun, but quite self-absorbed, and unlike my other 'supervising drivers', she took no notice of my driving whatsoever, just sat in the passenger seat and chatted away about her latest dating drama. I felt very relaxed and unselfconscious, even when it came to parking in a tight space outside the restaurant, and the experience gave my confidence a much-needed boost. *Georgia, 33*

6. Find the right driving instructor

When it comes to learning to drive, one of the most important decisions you will ever make is your choice of driving instructor. This subject is hugely important and one I've devoted a whole chapter to in my book *Driving Test Secrets You Need to Know*. This includes a step-by-step guide to tracking down the right instructor and also outlines potential 'red flags' for spotting instructors and driving schools which may have shady practices, such as offering lessons with an instructor who is a Potential Driving Instructor (PDI) rather than an Approved Driving Instructor (ADI) without informing you. PDIs are instructors who have achieved the driving part of their qualification, but haven't yet passed the tuition section. They are legally allowed to teach during this time, when working for a driving school rather than independently, but you should be made aware of their status and also of course pay less for their lessons than you would with an ADI. The chapter also covers other issues such as whether it's best to go with a large school or an independent instructor and your instructor's location.

My instructor Stacey was very good – and good-value too. I felt I'd lucked out with her. But then I read an article explaining the difference between an ADI and a PDI and during our next lesson I asked Stacey which she was. She looked embarrassed and said she was a PDI. She worked for a driving school and they hadn't told me when I booked in with her and she hadn't either. I looked at their website and they had a bit of background on each instructor and I noticed that Stacey and another instructor were less expensive than their colleagues and described as trainees, but it didn't clarify what that meant and the school hadn't mentioned it to me at the time of booking. I was near to my test so I stuck with Stacey as I felt she was a good instructor, but I did feel that both the school and she should have been upfront with me from the beginning.
Marcelle, 26

Bear in mind that not all instructors will suit everyone. Just because your petrol-head sister raves about her instructor, it doesn't mean you should automatically sign up with them. They might be an excellent instructor, but more suited to confident learners than nervous ones, for example. What's important is finding someone whose teaching techniques 'click' with you personally and with whom you feel comfortable sharing the ups and downs of your learning to drive journey.

I had to learn to drive in my 50s after my husband had a stroke. I was researching instructors on the internet and came across Mark, who ran his own automatic driving school. He looked so calm and friendly in his Facebook posts and his learners left such lovely comments I thought he might be the one for me – and he was! Learning to drive was an uphill struggle but Mark was an excellent teacher and so good at building up my confidence after my failed tests. I'm not sure I could have passed without him.
Jane, 58

When it comes to block-booking lessons in return for a discount, it's always best to find out whether you and a potential driving instructor suit each other first. You don't want to be locked into a relationship with an instructor which isn't really working because you need to 'use up' the lessons you've paid for. Wait until you know that they're right for you and then by all means take advantage of the savings.

2. Focus on your finances

There are few situations in life more guaranteed to drain your confidence than running out of money. Feeling that you've got to pass your driving test within a certain number of lessons means that each lesson is 'loaded'. The pressure you put on yourself to make rapid progress during your driving lessons can actually result in your progress being slower because you are too stressed to be fully open to learning. And then on driving test day the awareness that if you fail you're going to have to pay for another test and more lessons to keep your skills up to test standard can really ramp up anxiety levels.

When it comes to gaining their driving licence, it's difficult to separate out how much of the stress learners experience is because they're learning a complex skill, and how much is because of the financial strain they are up against, either because they are paying for their own lessons, or because they're worried about how much their parents or other family members are having to shell out.

Unless you (or your parents) are rolling in cash, the costs involved in gaining your driving licence can feel extremely daunting. But it's best to look them in the eye and budget accordingly. A common mistake learners make is to have a few hundred pounds they've saved from birthday money and other gifts, factor in the £70 a week that they earn from their Saturday job in a cafe and reckon that will be enough to see them through. But sadly, chances are it won't be. And then you could find yourself in the frustrating situation of having made progress with your lessons but needing to give them up because you've run out of money. Pausing your lessons then starting up again months later means your skills will have become rusty and you'll need more tuition to build them back up again than you would have if you'd been able to keep going.

> I learned to drive as a married mum of three young children and it was a very tight squeeze financially for us as a family.
> *Carla, 29*

I wanted to pass my test quickly because I was applying for jobs as a local newspaper reporter, all of which required a driving licence. I was taking 4 hours of lessons a week and spending hundreds of pounds a month. It was depressing as I felt I was living this painfully frugal lifestyle and if I ever had a difficult lesson where I struggled to concentrate and felt I'd made no progress I'd torture myself thinking of all the other things I could have spent the money on. *Marcelle, 26*

My partner Harry and I have been together since University and have always wanted to build up our savings and make good financial decisions. I was shocked at how much learning to drive depleted my savings, especially as personal reasons meant I had to stop and start my lessons several times, so the whole process was more expensive than it should have been. *Patrick, 32*

Apologies if all this is depressing (and confidence-depleting!) but it's important to have a realistic view of what you might need to spend and create a financial plan for getting your driving licence, ideally building up a decent buffer of cash before you begin.

Incidentally, I also want to flag up that it's important not to feel resentful about paying your instructor's fees. Bear in mind that a lot of the money doesn't go into their pocket, but goes towards their expenses, such as fuel costs, car maintenance and insurance, and also has to cover the time spent travelling between pupils.

In the UK the Driver and Vehicle Standards Agency (DVSA) reports that learners need on average 45 hours of lessons, together with at least 20 hours of private practice. Given that lessons cost between £40-50 an hour, you're looking at between £1800 and £2250. If you don't have a family car to practice in then that will likely mean you'll need more lessons and the process will cost more. You then need to factor in other costs such as your provisional licence, the theory test fees and learning materials, practical test fees, and insurance costs if you're doing private practice. And although you'll be hoping to breeze through your test first time, the fact is that only 48% of candidates manage this. If you're not one of them then that means paying for more lessons to maintain your skills, together with more test fees.

If your parents are paying for or contributing to your lessons it's good to get an idea of how much they are OK with spending. Some parents can comfortably cough up for an infinite number of driving lessons and treat their offspring to a brand-new car for their 17th birthday into the bargain. But the majority will have a far more limited budget and need to prioritise important household bills over getting you on the road. Talking with them about costs right at the beginning is important, especially as they may well not realise how many lessons are likely to be required. The driving test has become more difficult than it was 30, 20 or even 10 years ago and they will probably have needed far fewer lessons to pass it than you will. I go into this topic in more detail later in this book, in a section describing how The driving test has become more difficult to pass, so be sure to show it to your parents or any older relatives or friends who are keen to tell you about how quickly they passed and don't understand why you need more lessons.

How many lessons you personally might need is going to depend on various factors. The most important is your natural driving ability, but other factors such as age and confidence levels are also significant. When you've had several lessons, ask your instructor how many they feel you might need so you'll have a rough idea of whether you're likely to require more or fewer lessons than average, and can budget accordingly.

When you're creating your budget, it can be a good idea to spend time thinking of ways you can generate extra income, and also decide what cutbacks will be the least painful.

> I was a student but had an extra job in a call centre to earn money for my lessons. I chose it because it offered the best hourly rate, but it was very stressful as I had to deal with angry customers. A couple of years later I was at University and working part -time at a bar. It was a fun environment and many of my colleagues became friends. If I had my time again, I'd have chosen to do a more enjoyable job at a lower rate to pay for my lessons. It might have meant working more hours, but at least they wouldn't have been miserable ones. *Nathan, 25*

I decided to cut back on clothes and eating out when I was learning to drive. I made the best of what I already had in my wardrobe and suggested to friends that we meet for coffee rather than dinner. I also asked my family if we could just do token gifts that year, as I felt too skint to buy proper Christmas presents. *Marcelle, 26*

CHAPTER 3

8 WAYS TO BOOST YOUR DRIVING CONFIDENCE

1. Use some simple strategies to avoid left-right confusion

When your instructor tells you to 'take the next available left turn', do you have a second's hesitation as you work out which way they mean? If so you're not alone, as right-left confusion is very common.

According to a Dutch study reported in The Quarterly Journal of Experimental Psychology in 2020, 14.6% of people report difficulties in telling their left from their right. Many interviewees didn't have a strategy for dealing with this, but some did. 13% would remind themselves by flexing their hands and seeing that the left hand makes an 'L' with the thumb and index finger, 28% would work it out through remembering which was their writing hand, whilst 1% used jewellery as a prompt, for example wearing a 'ring on their right hand'. 10% reported using 'another strategy', which they had developed for themselves. If you have a problem with left-right confusion, then playing around with a few different techniques until you find one that works will help you feel more confident.

I do Irish set dance and have always had a problem with telling my left from my right.

> During classes I would wear a watch on my left hand, and a red bracelet on my right, so watch = left and red = right. I used the same strategy in my driving lessons and it definitely helped, especially with parking manoeuvres. *Maura, 25*

It might seem like I'm pointing out the obvious, but it's really important to note the word 'available' in the phrase 'take the next available left turn'. Plenty of nervous learners have just taken the next left turn and found themselves in the parking area of a scrapyard or car home.

> My driving instructor asked me to take the next available left turn and I saw what looked like a lane coming up so I took it, only to realise that was leading to the grounds of a large hotel – I'd just not spotted the sign. I was annoyed with myself as I'm an experienced motor cyclist and felt I should have noticed. *Rowan, 23*

2. Breathe

The main benefit of breathing is that it keeps us alive. However there are times when it works for us more effectively than others. For example, if we are tense our breathing can become constricted, which can then make us feel even more anxious. However keeping your breathing more relaxed can encourage both your body and mind to believe that everything is fine. This calms you down and means you will perform better and have an improved chance of passing your driving test – a powerful incentive to learn and practice breathing techniques!

The best approach is to start experimenting with breathing exercises well in advance of your driving test. Experimenting with different breathing techniques before your lessons means you'll learn more effectively and by the time your driving test rolls round you'll already know what works best for you.

Here are some possible approaches:

You could try downloading a breathing app which will offer techniques to help you deepen and relax your breathing.

Or you could just sit quietly and focus on your breath. Don't try to change it in any way, just observe it initially. As you do so you could mentally say a word or phrase such as 'relax' or 'I am calm'. Do this for five minutes to start with, and increase the time if possible.

Sometimes it can be helpful to lie down on the floor. Obviously this won't be an option in the driving test waiting room, but it can give you a deeper experience of relaxation and your ability to slow down and soften your breath. Find somewhere comfortable, use a pillow if necessary and cover yourself with a blanket. Then repeat the process outlined above. Also, let yourself really feel the way the floor beneath you is giving you its support and relax into it. Say to yourself, 'I am always safe and supported'.

Exercises that involve counting the breath can be helpful – for example breathing in gently for a count of 5, and then releasing the breath slowly for a count of 5.

There are lots of variations when it comes to timing your breathing, such as the 4-4-4 technique, which involves breathing in for four counts, holding your breath for four counts and then exhaling for four counts.

Then there's the 4-7-8 technique. For this you inhale to the count of four, hold your breath for seven counts then exhale for eight.

Or you could just hold an image in your mind of a candle, or a mountain or clouds scudding across the sky – anything that makes you feel calm and safe will help soften and relax your breathing. Try different approaches as one that might work brilliantly for one person would be boring or annoying for another. Through trial and error you'll be sure to find a technique that works for you.

I've done yoga for decades and learned the 4-7-8 technique which the teacher said was called Kumbhaka Pranayama. It's my favourite breathing method for relaxation and I used it before my lessons and tests.
Jane, 58

I've tried meditation techniques that involve counting my breath and hated them. They just seemed boring and as if I was doing a job. Then I heard about a technique where you 'breathe through your heart' – imagining that your heart is doing the breathing rather than your lungs. I loved it and do it regularly now. As well as being relaxing it gives me a warm, positive feeling. I tried to do it in the driving test waiting room before both my tests. It was challenging because the atmosphere was very tense and I felt I was picking up the anxieties of all the other candidates, as well as my own. But the 'breathing through my heart' technique' did help me in detach a bit and I felt I was able to be within a 'calmer bubble' of my own. I failed my first test, but I did pass the second and I think using that combined meditation and breathing technique helped. *Millie, 27*

3. Tweak your inner dialogue

If you've ever read any self-help books, you'll be aware of the significance of observing and upgrading your inner monologue. For example, if you're trying to lose weight, thoughts such as *'I promised myself I'd go to the gym after work but when Sam suggested we all go out for drinks I skipped it. There's no point in trying to get fit, I'm too lazy and weak-willed'*, aren't particularly helpful. It's better to replace them with more positive ones along the lines of *'Maybe I should exercise before work instead, then I know it's sorted'*, or *'To be honest I hate the gym and I'll take any excuse to get out of it. If I find an exercise I enjoy I'll be more likely to stick to it. I'll give swimming and dance classes a try.'*

So now take that basic principle and apply to various learning to drive and driving test scenarios and see how much better you feel. There are a couple of examples below, but this technique works best when you adapt it to your own experiences and feelings.

Driving lesson thoughts upgrade

1. *My last driving lesson was a complete disaster. I made so many stupid mistakes,and it's not as if I'm a beginner any more. I've had 30 lessons and I should be better than this by now. I'm probably the worst pupil my instructor Danielle has ever had, but she's too kind to say so.*

2. *My last driving lesson didn't go brilliantly. I thought I'd really got the hang of reversing round a corner, but today I mounted the kerb on both attempts. It was like I'd forgotten everything I'd been taught. But my driving instructor was calm and encouraging and just explained the manoeuvre to me again until I finally got it right. I felt a bit embarrassed given that I've had 30 lessons. But the thing to remember about driving instructors is that they're unshockable – after more than 25 years as an instructor I bet Danielle has seen it all!*

Driving test thoughts upgrade

1. *It's my second driving test today and I'm so worried that I'm going to fail again. I'll have to pay for more lessons and another test, and learning to drive has cost me a fortune already. What if I get the same examiner as I did last time? He was so quiet and I don't think he liked me. I bet he'd really enjoy failing me again.*

2. *It's my second driving test today and I just know I'm going to pass this time. Loads of people fail their first test because of nerves, and that's what happened with me. But now I know what to expect I'll be a lot more confident and that means I'll drive better. My driving instructor Henry believes in me and I've already passed mock tests with him so I know I can do it. And it doesn't matter which examiner I get. My*

instructor told me that all driving examiners have to have the same pass rates as their colleagues at the test centre and that there's no such thing as 'that nasty examiner who fails everyone'. He also said that driving examiners have to treat everyone the same, so some of them can come across as a bit formal. It's nothing personal. If I do get the same examiner that I did for my last test he'll see how much I've improved and be sure to pass me.

4. Remember that driving test standards are higher than they've ever been

One of the problems around learning to drive is that parents and older relatives often express surprise and disappointment that today's learners need so many lessons. This is especially the case when it comes complaining about paying for them!

Feeling that you're a slower learner than older family members has the potential to dent your confidence. But the need for more lessons isn't because the younger generation are in any way less capable at the wheel than their parents were – quite the reverse in fact. It's because the driving test has become far more demanding in recent decades and the standard required to pass is extremely high. This is to reflect the fact that roads are busier and more complex, and also to ensure that learners have a solid grounding in all the necessary skills and attitudes to become a safe driver.

So many extra elements have been included that that anyone passing the test now will be required to demonstrate a much higher level of competence than candidates back in the day. If you want proof, I'd suggest you check out any YouTube videos about driving in the 1960s or even 1980s. One video, entitled In-Car Camera London to Bath 1963 is especially fascinating. Mr G Eyles of the Institute of Advanced Motoring drives a route going through towns such as Reading, Newbury and Chippenham, encountering very little traffic and by today's standards no complicated road junctions whatsoever.

Here's a brief history of the UK driving test, so you can see how it has evolved.

June 1935

Driving tests began the UK. There weren't any test centres so examiners would meet candidates at a pre-arranged place such as a bus station or village hall. The test cost seven shillings and sixpence, or 37p, which is the equivalent of £33 in 2024. The current cost of the practical driving test is £62. The pass rate back then was 63%, compared to around 48% in recent years.

1939-1947

Driving tests were suspended during WW2 in the UK and provisional licence owners were allowed to drive independently. For a year following the end of the war the provisional licences could be converted into full licences without the need for a practical test – which means that some motorists of that generation never took a single lesson or a test.

1958

The first stretch of motorway in the UK was built – the M6 Preston Bypass

1990

It became a legal requirement that anyone supervising a learner driver should have held a licence for three years and be 21 or over.

April 1991

For the first time a reverse parking manoeuvre became a compulsory part of the test. Many motorists who passed before this date might not have had much formal training in parking skills.

July 1996

A written Theory Test was introduced. Before this the examiner would ask some Highway Code questions at the end of the test, and even if the candidate got them wrong it would only count as a minor fault and they would still pass. Candidates need to pass their theory test before they can take the practical one.

June 1997

The New Driver Act came into force. It means that any new driver who gets six or more penalty points in their first two years of driving loses their licence and has to take their theory and practical tests again. Many learners aren't aware of this particular piece of legislation but it's something you should take very seriously indeed.

January 2002

The first touch-screen Theory Test was introduced.

November 2002

The Hazard Perception section was added to the Theory Test

September 2003

The Show me/Tell Me car safety questions were added to the beginning of the practical test

April 2010

Since this date driving test candidates have been encouraged to be accompanied by their driving instructor on their test, though it's not necessary and remains a matter of personal choice.

October 2010

A ten minute 'independent driving' section was introduced to the test.

December 2017

A number of important changes to the driving test were brought in. These included:

- Increasing the 'independent driving' section from 10 to 20 minutes – almost half of the test
- The use of a sat nav. Candidates need to be able to follow directions from a sat nav, as they are now used in four out of five tests. The remaining one out of five requires the candidate to follow traffic signs instead
- The 'reversing around a corner' and 'turn in the road' manoeuvres no longer form part of the test, though they should be taught by instructors. Instead candidates are asked to do one out of three manoeuvres – parallel park, bay park or pull up on the right-hand side of the road, reverse for two car lengths and then rejoin the traffic

- Two vehicle safety questions, known as the 'show me, tell me' questions are asked. The 'tell me' question (where you are asked a safety question at the start of the test before you start driving) and the 'show me' question, (where you are asked a safety question while driving). If you get one or both questions wrong you will get a minor fault.

June 2018

Learner drivers became able to take motorway lessons when accompanied by an ADI in a dual-controlled car.

As you can see, a candidate in 1990 wouldn't have needed to show they could reverse park, drive independently or answer any safety questions. They wouldn't have had to take a theory test, just answer a few Highway Code questions and if they'd got them wrong it would have just meant a minor fault, so they would still have passed.

If you're reading this and wish that your driving test could be that easy – don't. Although a lot is being asked of you right now, you will get through it and become a better, safer driver in the long run. Probably much better than your parents or grandparents, though it would be more tactful not to mention that to them....

When I was teaching back in the late 1960s, I could get most people through in 10 to 15 lessons. That would be completely impossible these days and rightly so. Roundabouts and junctions are extremely busy and the speed and volume of traffic creates challenging situations requiring very accurate judgement. For example, back then you would usually only have one set of traffic lights at a junction, whereas now there might be several sets, together with complex filtration systems. *Eddie, retired driving instructor, 86*

I was surprised when my daughter Alex said she didn't need to do a turn in the road on her driving test. That was the very first manoeuvre I got the hang of. It didn't take me long to learn and I got it right, including the observations every time. Bay parking was a different matter, mind you. I think the turn in the road is a very useful manoeuvre and something drivers will use far more frequently than that new one which involves reversing two car lengths. *Luis, 50*

I was born at the beginning of WW2. After the war, there was a test backlog and people who'd been driving on a provisional licence could just convert it to a full one without ever taking a test. There were adults in my family had never taken a driving lesson or test. As far as test standards and road safety goes, I grew up in a very different era. It wasn't even compulsory to wear a seatbelt till 1983, when I was in my mid-forties.

I come from a large family where the oldest sibling was taught by our father, and then when that sibling had passed they were meant to teach the younger one and so on down the ranks. I was the youngest so there had probably been a lot of bad habits passed on by then. When I turned up for my driving test I expected to pass and was shocked when I didn't. Apparently I'd gone significantly over the speed limit, which I hadn't even noticed. Had to deal with a lot of ribbing from my brothers – my father gave me some top up lessons and I passed second time.

By the time our children were grown up the test was a lot more demanding and my wife and I realised it was going to cost a lot of money to get our daughters on the road. We were willing to cough up though, as we both feel that driving is an important skill and gives you so much freedom. All the girls passed easily apart from Chloe. Privately we thought she'd never crack it but she just wouldn't give up. She always was a very determined girl. I'm in my 80s now and my wife Hilary is in her 70s. I've been diagnosed with cataracts and have had to give up driving, and Hilary has become less confident behind the wheel and will only do short distances, such as into the nearest village. Chloe has moved out of London and now lives much closer to our home in the Cotswolds, and her help in driving us when we need to go longer distances has been invaluable. To be honest, I don't know how we'd manage without her. *Simon, 85*

I'm in my 60s, took my driving test at 17 and passed first time. I wasn't at all confident, but learning to drive was much easier back then. The roads were quieter and in the 1970s you didn't even have to do a reverse parking manoeuvre during your test. I can't even remember being taught them. Because the standard was much lower we didn't need as many lessons to pass, so learning to drive was more affordable. I paid for it with my Saturday job wages and some birthday money. Although I was pleased to get my licence, I do feel it would have been better for me to have had more in-depth training when I was younger. I hate going anywhere where I'm not sure about the parking, as I've never done a bay or reverse park in my life. I can only drive in and out of parking spaces like the supermarket. And if I'm visiting friends who live in terraced houses, I often have to park a long way away. I've also never driven on a motorway and now I don't suppose I ever shall. I am confident driving on narrow roads and challenging weather conditions however – as I'm born and bred in North Wales I've had plenty of practice at both! My daughter Sian took eight attempts to pass her driving test. She always was a worrier and struggled with exams at school for that reason. So when it came to the driving test all those anxieties returned. I'm so proud of her for not giving up. She's a much better driver than I am now

– she can get into the tightest spaces and has driven up and down the UK and even driven abroad which I can't even imagine myself attempting.

Sian says I should take some top-up lessons to help me with parking, but I've always felt it would be too embarrassing. But then a friend of mine is learning from scratch in her 50s and says her instructor is lovely and supportive so I have been wondering if I might take some extra lessons with him. It would be wonderful not to have to worry about parking the way I do now.
Rebecca, 64

I was learning to drive in 1990, and I knew that reverse parking was going to be brought in as part of the driving test in 1991. My driving instructor taught me the manoeuvres but my success with them was very hit-and-miss. I was desperate to pass before they were introduced into the test. I had two tests beforehand, which I failed and my next test was after completing a parking manoeuvre was made compulsory. I messed up the bay park on my third test, but I would have failed it anyway, because I also got a major fault for hesitating too much at a junction. I got bay parking again on my fourth test, and no other faults, so I finally passed. My partner Fiona and I live in Edinburgh where there's very little parking, and

I often have to squeeze into tight spots, so although spending all that time and money on extra lessons wasn't something I'd have wanted at the time, it's been very worthwhile in the long run. *Grace, 56*

5. Tailor your social media scrolling for driving test success

If, like most people you feel spend too much time on social media, why not decide you're going to at least make it more productive? Rather than just scrolling mindlessly when you're waiting in a queue or on public transport, adjust your feed so you can pick up extra driving test tips in your spare time. TikTok offers short videos with advice from successful learners and driving instructors, whilst on YouTube you can watch lessons and mock tests carried out by qualified instructors, and also view some driving test routes complete with commentary. Forums like Reddit give you the opportunity to connect with other learners and driving instructors. They're a great place to share your experiences, ask for advice and get support.

And don't just stick to driving-related videos – general ones on goal-setting and confidence-boosting can work well too.

I would never have passed the Hazard Perception part of my theory test without help from YouTube videos – I had the official materials, and they were OK, but I kept clicking in the wrong place and didn't understand why. There are some YouTubers who are also driving instructors or driving experts who run channels helping with the Theory Test and they give in-depth explanations about when you should click and why, so I finally understood what the test was looking for. *Carla, 29*

I follow some YouTubers who give advice on fitness and having a positive mindset. I would watch their videos after a difficult lesson and they would help me stay committed to learning to drive. *Dan, 18*

6. Go on a 'road trip'

Although a 'trip to the supermarket' is the bread and butter of private practice, it's good to upgrade sometimes to scones and cake. What I mean by that is that it can boost both your confidence and your mood to do some fun driving. Yes, actual fun. Not bracing yourself to tackle a busy dual carriageway. Not completing a few bay parks in a rainy, deserted car park. But instead upgrading your private practice by planning and going on an enjoyable outing with your supervising companion. The distance and complexity of this journey will of course vary depending on how experienced and confident you've become.

A 'road trip' taken relatively early in your learning to drive journey will differ from one shortly before your test. But to get the maximum value out of your outing it's important that you should take on the role of driver as much as possible – by which I mean do the safety checks before setting off, plan your route, and take responsibility for finding parking and fuelling the vehicle. Just like you will when you're a licensed driver.

It was the school holidays and I asked my mum if she'd take me out for a practice drive. She agreed and then said, 'let's be ladies who lunch!' and suggested that we go to a historic house with a tearoom about 30 minutes drive away. I'd been there as a passenger in the back seat lots of times but I realised I must never have been paying proper attention to the route as I wasn't sure what turnings to take. I looked them up on a map beforehand so there wouldn't be any problems with finding the way. I drove my mum to the house and when we arrived I was happy to see there was plenty of space in the car park so that was very straightforward. The weather was beautiful so after a lovely lunch we walked around the gardens together and I drove her home. When my dad and brother got back from work she told them how well I'd done and they were really pleased. I'd already failed three tests at that point and my confidence was very low. It was only my determination to get my licence so I could eventually do my dream job of being a warden on a nature reserve that was keeping me going. That outing really cheered me up. I still failed my next test, but I passed the fifth. It was one of the happiest days of my life! The following weekend our whole family went to the historic house for lunch to celebrate and I drove us there and back! *Kira, 19*

My parents are divorced but my dad lives locally and we see a lot of each other. Shortly before my first driving test we'd planned to have a surfing weekend together near St Ives in Cornwall. The route from Exmoor, where we live is over 130 miles but doesn't involve any motorways, so I could drive it all myself. We decided that although he would be supervising me, I would take responsibility for the trip. I planned the route and loaded up the car with all our camping and surfing gear. Then I did the safety checks, ensuring that the tyre pressure was correct, bearing in mind the extra load the car was carrying. My dad just sat in the house while I was doing all that, drinking a cup of tea – though he did double-check everything before we set off. The weather was very bad during the journey out, and my dad asked if I was still OK with driving and I said yes. I'd been out in stormy weather with my instructor before, so I felt confident. We got to the campsite, set up our tent and after that first night, the weather and surf were fantastic. I drove us down to the beach and back every day. It felt just like being a licensed driver. The only things that were different were that neither of us could have a drink in the pub, as I was driving and as supervising driver, my dad was legally in charge of the car, so we both needed to avoid alcohol. But we just had a beer back at the campsite instead. Then there was one time when we needed something from the village shop, and I said I'd go. If I'd passed my test I could have gone alone, but of course this time my dad had to accompany me. It was a brilliant weekend, and one I'll always remember. *Fergus, 20*

7. Congratulate yourself!

If you delay celebrating yourself and your achievements until you've finally torn up your L plates, learning to drive may well feel like a long and dispiriting journey.

To keep your spirits up and motivation high, it's important to set yourself mini-goals and acknowledge and congratulate yourself for achieving them along the way.

Your mini-goals can be directly related to driving, such as when you execute your first successful reverse park. Or they can be about tackling a problem, such as moving on from an instructor you're not suited to and finding another with whom you 'click' much better.

Celebrating even the smallest success can help positively transform your feelings about learning to drive. For example, if you've just completed a focused session revising for your theory test (without veering off onto social media), make a nice hot drink, and as the kettle is boiling say to yourself, 'I've just finished a really good session, well done! Or if you've done your first supervised practice drive to the supermarket without any prompting, allow yourself a smug grin and a warm glow of pride. When your driving instructor says you're ready to take your test, this is definitely a time for you to blast out some music and do your 'victory dance' (though it's best to wait until you get home before you actually start busting some moves, obviously).

And don't just congratulate yourself for your 'successes'. Even something goes wrong, such as failing a test, you still deserve to congratulate yourself for the effort you put in, and for being brave enough to try.

You can congratulate yourself in lots of different ways. For example, by saying positive words, by smiling and giving yourself a thumbs-up in the mirror, or treating yourself to a coffee at your favourite cafe or a bunch of flowers. You could even give yourself a round of applause!

I work in PR and am mostly remote these days. I enjoy being at home and being able to walk our dog Norman at lunchtime, but I do miss the office sometimes, especially when I land good media coverage for a client, but there's no-one around to share the good news with. A colleague once said that when he worked at home and something went well, he'd give himself a round of applause. I thought that was a great idea and started doing it myself. Anyway, once when my partner Jake and I had come back from a session of driving practice that went well, I started clapping myself, and explained why. He laughed and joined in and after that it became a ritual for us both to clap after driving practice. It felt a bit silly, but also fun and it always boosted my mood. *Millie, 27*

8. Have a mock test

Or better yet, have several. A mock test is where your instructor incorporates a full 'driving test' into your lesson. It will begin just as a real test would, with an eyesight test and the 'show me, tell me' checks and then go through all the other components with your instructor acting the role of examiner. Some examiners enlist colleagues to give that part of the lesson and act the role of the 'examiner' for a more authentic experience. Mock tests are hugely helpful and I strongly recommend that you have at least one before your official test.

I had several mock tests before my real test and I did find them useful. I didn't pass all of them and when my instructor Ravi told me I'd failed one I was very disappointed. But I passed the others and to hear someone say those magic words, 'That's the end of the test and I'm pleased to say you've passed' meant a lot to me. *Maura, 25*

CHAPTER 4

STAYING ON TRACK

1. Be where you are. It will all make sense later

Learning any new skill has its up and downs, and driving can be particularly daunting as you're aware of what a high standard you will be required to reach. At the beginning (or even in the middle) it can seem as if you'll never get there. It's common to experience a 'learning plateau' where the initial progress you've made flattens out and you feel as if you're not getting any better. But this is a totally normal phenomenon – you're just gradually integrating the complex skills that you are being taught. Eventually they will become more natural and you will experience upward progress. Just focus on what you are currently learning and trust that everything will come together in the end.

> Not long after starting my driving lessons I was on the top deck of a bus going over a flyover. I looked down and beneath me I could see these busy and complex road junctions and roundabouts. My heart sank, my mind froze and my stomach turned over with fright. I remember thinking, 'I'm never going to be able to cope with that sort of traffic, it's scary and complicated

and everyone is going too fast. I'm just not capable'. But by taking it step-by-step with my lovely instructor Amanda I did get there in the end. I still don't especially like unfamiliar busy junctions and I don't suppose I ever will, but I can handle them. *Joanne, 48*

2. You don't have to be a 'star pupil'

If you're academically bright and good at written exams, but are finding learning to drive a struggle – this one's for you! Because of your natural aptitude for the particular type of learning that's required in schools and universities, you have probably developed a perception of yourself as someone who 'picks things up easily' Which is all very well when it's about analysing *The Merchant of Venice*, or getting to grips with quadratic equations.

But learning to drive requires different skills, such as the ability to judge speed and distance, and good co-ordination. This is why you may have mates who don't excel in exams but pass their driving test first time, no minors and no worries. Because driving is something they are naturally good at.

And if you're not, and it takes you longer to learn, that's OK. Let go of the idea of being a 'Star Pupil' and accept that this is an area in which you might need more tuition and support than others. It's not something to feel ashamed of, any more than someone who has dyslexia or a physical disability should feel bad about needing extra help.

Of course, the pressure around being a 'Star Pupil' might not just come from you, but from others. Family expectations can be a hurdle, especially if you have parents and older siblings who passed easily. And then of course there are particular driving instructors who are very preoccupied with their 'high first-time pass rate'. These tend to be instructors whose pupils are mostly young, confident and pass easily. When they flag up their high first-time pass rate on their website and social media, that attracts more of those pupils and of course also appeals to parents who want to get their teens on the road as safely and inexpensively as possible. If they then take on a pupil who struggles with learning and also with driving test nerves, then it's going to swiftly dawn on them they might not get a first-time pass and this pupil could bring down their rating. But even if an instructor does have these concerns, it's important that they should keep them very much to themselves and not let any pupil feel 'less than' because they need more tuition and support. If you have an ongoing sense that your instructor views you as 'a disappointment' then it's time to move on to another instructor who will appreciate and respect you.

> Most of my pupils are between 17-21 and I've got a very good first time pass rate, not every pupil is successful straight away – sometimes they find the test situation very challenging. I had one young learner, Kira, who took five attempts to pass and I was so proud of her when she did. As driving instructors, it's our responsibility to do our best for every pupil regardless of their level of ability. *Emily 28, driving instructor*

> I'm the youngest of five children. I have an older brother and three sisters. They all took lessons in sixth form, passed their driving

tests easily and everyone, myself included, thought I would too. But I could not get the hang of a manual car, and was still licence-less when I left home for university. I had to deal with my siblings' teasing, which was annoying, and my parents disappointment, which was much worse. It wasn't until I was working in Cardiff and switched to learning on an automatic car that I finally managed to pass my test. *Rukmini, 33*

I'm one of three children and my parents are keen for us all to be high-achievers. We're expected to get great grades, be sporty and musical and pass our driving tests early and easily. It's a lot of pressure. *Octavia, 18*

3. Being self-reliant will build your driving test confidence

An important life-lesson is that sometimes people don't do what they say they will, especially when it involves spending their time or money. So even if partners or family members make promises about paying for lessons or taking you out practising, don't take their offer too seriously until it's clear that it's something they'll actually do, rather than flake out on.

My uncle always said for years that he'd take me out practising, but when the time came he was always 'too busy'. *Ashley, 18*

Also, sometimes sincere offers of help are made, but then circumstances change for perfectly understandable reasons and you just have to make other arrangements.

> I've got a really good friend who said she'd take me out for driving practice. But then she got pregnant and was told it was a high-risk pregnancy and she had to be extra careful. Understandably it wouldn't have been a good idea for her to be in a car driven by a learner driver. I just accepted that I'd just have to take extra lessons. *Carla, 29*

When it comes to money matters, it's easy for wires to get crossed, so if anyone offers you financial help with lessons, it's a good idea to clarify exactly what they mean, even if it feels a bit awkward.

> My grandparents are very well-off and they always said they'd pay for my driving lessons. They gave my parents enough money to pay for the first six, but then didn't offer any more, even though it was obvious it was taking me loads of lessons. My parents had assumed that they meant they would pay for all the costs up to and including as many tests as I needed, but then it dawned on them that wasn't the case. It felt awkward and although I'm grateful to my grandparents it would have been better if they'd been clear about how much money they were willing to give. Thankfully I passed first time, so at least my parents only had to pay for one test. *Sabrina, 19*

And then there's the possibility that you might be the one who wants to turn down the original offer, because taking it up doesn't seem right for whatever reason.

> I failed my first test and then went home over the festive break. My second test was booked for the new year, and I wanted to keep my skills up so when my dad suggested he take me out for some practice sessions I agreed. But he's over 80 now, and only does very limited journeys to familiar destinations like the supermarket. When we actually went out together I could tell that he was nervous so I said I was worried I might pick up bad habits without my instructor Danielle there to supervise me, and that I'd have extra lessons with her instead. Dad didn't want to admit it, but I could tell he was relieved. *Jacob, 42*

When you're learning to drive, it's great if you've got family, friends or a partner who will support you, whether that's financially, emotionally or by taking you out practising. But be aware that things might not always work out as planned, and trust that you'll find other solutions. Taking a self-reliant attitude towards learning will help build your confidence, not just as a driver, but in your future life.

4. When your driving instructor moves on

Not every learner driver-instructor relationship 'clicks'. If you don't feel you're making progress with a particular instructor then it's important to address any problems or change to a different instructor. Staying with an instructor who's not right for you will make the process of learning to drive longer, more stressful and more expensive.

But sometimes it's not the learner who moves on, or has to pause or cancel lessons, but the instructor. This could be down to a variety of very valid reasons such as ill-health, family problems, taking parental leave, moving to another part of the country, career change or retirement.

Good driving instructors care about their pupils, and want to offer you consistency all the way from your first lesson to a successful test pass. Unfortunately that isn't always possible, though if it's something that involves advance planning, such as moving away from the area, they'll hopefully give you plenty of notice.

Your departing instructor might suggest someone, and by all means have a trial lesson with them, but don't feel obliged to stick with the new instructor if they don't feel a good fit for whatever reason. There's a detailed chapter on Finding the Right Driving Instructor in my book *Driving Test Secrets You Need to Know*, that you might find helpful.

If you've got a good relationship with your instructor and they have to stop teaching you then it's understandable that you're going to be upset. The prospect of getting used to someone new can be daunting and affect your confidence, especially if you're close to your driving test. But life doesn't always go smoothly and although you might prefer to stay with your original instructor, it's important to remember that you don't 'need' them to become a good and safe driver and pass your test. There are plenty of quality instructors that can get you through.

What if my driving instructor has to pause my lessons?

Good driving instructors will always try to keep your lessons consistent, but like everyone, there will be times when they have important personal issues to deal with. If your driving instructor needs to take a temporary break then it's your decision whether to wait for them to return, or to move on to a new instructor.

> Five years ago my mother was terminally ill. I had to take time off and return to the family home in Scotland and help care for her. When I left the Lake District I had no idea how long I'd be gone so I couldn't give my students a clear idea of when I'd be available for lessons again. I know all the local instructors, and there are plenty I would wholeheartedly recommend so I did my best to help my learners find replacement instructors while I was away. When I returned a few months later some had already passed their tests. I contacted the others to let them know I was back and that I'd be happy to teach them again, but also that I'd fully understand if they would prefer to stay with their new instructor. Some returned to me and others didn't, and I respected their choices. It was a very difficult time, both personally and professionally and I really appreciate the consideration and understanding my learners showed. *Danielle, 56*

Don't take being ghosted personally

Some learners might experience an unprofessional instructor who 'ghosts' them – that is, cancels or doesn't turn up for lessons and doesn't reply to your messages. If this happens to you your first thought might be that the instructor is ill or having personal problems – but if a quick check of their social media reveals they are still teaching, then clearly something is up. Try reaching them through a few different means, in case there's a communications glitch such as your email bouncing. Don't worry that this makes you look stalker-ish. If they have decided not to teach you any more for any reason, they have a responsibility to inform you themselves. Ghosting is inexcusable. If you've paid for any lessons in advance, it's important that you get your money back. You will also need your Driver's Record, which is your progress report. Inform the instructor that if they don't refund any money owing and send any necessary paperwork you'll report them to the DVSA.

Whether it's dating or driving-related, being ghosted is a horrible experience. It can leave the 'ghostee' feeling emotionally bruised and even wondering if their driving instructor just couldn't stand being around them, or if they were too hopeless for them to teach. But put thoughts like that firmly out of your mind. This is very much a 'it's not you, it's them' scenario. Because whatever their reason for ending your lessons, it's their responsibility as an instructor to explain why, rather than do a disappearing act because they want to avoid an awkward conversation. Sometimes an instructor might realise that they don't have the ability to teach a particular learner. They might not have the skills to cope with someone with dyspraxia, or who has severe anxiety, for example. But that's not an acceptable reason to abandon them without explanation.

Also, bear in mind it's extremely likely that the reason you've been 'dumped' has absolutely nothing to do with your driving or who you are as a person. Maybe it's just that you live somewhere that's not that convenient for the instructor to get to. They might have taken you on because they needed the work at the time, but now they're booked up and want to offload you. Or maybe they're just plain flaky. Who knows?

I was learning with one of the big driving schools and had been assigned an Australian guy called Seth. I had a few lessons with him and we got on well. Then out of the blue I got a message from the driving school saying that Seth wasn't available any more and that another instructor would be teaching me instead. I don't know what had happened with Seth. Maybe he'd gone back to Australia or decided he didn't want to be a driving instructor any more. Seth had never mentioned anything to me about leaving and at the end of our last lesson he'd said, 'see you next week' – so it was a total mystery! I had one lesson with the new guy, and we didn't click that well so my parents decided to book me lessons with an instructor who had his own independent school locally. They felt that he would have worked hard to build up his reputation and short of ill-health or family problems he

would stick with me till I passed, which he
did. *Dan, 18*

A blessing in disguise?

Of course, having your driving instructor move on isn't
always a disaster. If the relationship isn't working it can
be an opportunity to start again with a new instructor and
a fresh attitude. Also, if you're close to your test the experience of driving with someone different can be helpful.

My instructor Pete was a lovely guy, but we'd
got into this awkward situation where he'd
repeatedly explain things, but not in ways
I could understand. Eventually I'd pretend
I'd got it because I was embarrassed and
didn't want to hurt his feelings. But then the
next lesson I'd be just as clueless because I
hadn't really learned anything. Pete and his
wife Magda both worked part-time so they
could share childcare. Her shifts changed
which meant Pete couldn't teach me on
Tuesdays any more, and that was the only
day I had available so our lessons had to end.
I pretended to be sad when he told me but
inside I was relieved. I'd wanted to move
on from him for ages but hadn't plucked
up courage to say so. When I got inside
my house I did a happy dance! I realised
that I could make a fresh start with a new
instructor and promised myself I wouldn't
make the same mistake again – I would

always be honest with them about what I did and didn't understand'. *Georgia, 33*

I took a year off between school and University and wanted to learn to drive with Gavin, a lovely older instructor who had taught a lot of my friends. Gavin explained that he was planning on retiring in a year's time, but I thought it didn't matter as I would have already passed. But then I had an accident and broke my arm, which meant I couldn't drive for a while, and all the time we were getting closer to Gavin's retirement date. I was hoping he'd carry on with my lessons just to get me through my test. But then he mentioned he and his partner James had booked a round-the-world cruise. Obviously they weren't going to be putting that off just for me! I did take one test with Gavin, but I failed it. He went off on his dream holiday and I had to switch to another instructor, Cheryl. It felt very strange to be learning with someone else. Cheryl was fine, but I still missed Gavin. I'd got very comfortable with him and felt he knew my driving strengths and weak spots inside out. On the plus side, lessons with Cheryl got me used to driving with someone unfamiliar, so when I had my second test I wasn't self-conscious in front of the examiner the way I had been the first time and passed. *Kim, 22*

It's understandable that learners can come to rely on their driving instructors, both for their teaching skills and the emotional support they offer.

> When I find someone who can look after me properly I really bond with them and no-one else will do. As far as I'm concerned, Mr Powell is the best dentist ever, only Erica can cut my hair and no-one but Ravi can teach me to drive. I'd have been so upset if he'd moved or retired before I'd passed my test, but thankfully he didn't!
> *Maura, 25*

But try not to see your driving instructor moving on as a major disaster. Focus on keeping your spirits and confidence levels up and tracking down one of the many other kind, capable instructors who can help you.

Making a smooth transition

Your previous driving instructor will have kept a record of your progress, which should be passed on to your new instructor. As well as the official records, it's a good idea to give your instructor a personal insight into your feelings and experiences about driving. The more information you can give them the better, whether it's about your challenges with handling a particular junction or how your private practice is progressing. The more they know about your driving history and you as a person, the more able they will be to help you and the more smoothly your change to your new instructor will be.

5. Don't be discouraged by other people's opinions

It's easy to fall into the trap of stereotyping people. This often happens in families where one sibling is seen as 'the arty one' and another as 'the practical one'. Usually it's done without much thought and can even be well-meaning. But difficulties can arise when learners have their confidence knocked because family, friends or colleagues imply that they're 'too scatty', 'too anxious', 'too old' or some other issue, to become a safe and capable driver.

Don't be influenced by what other people think you can or can't do. Their opinions of you are just their opinions and you don't need to be limited by them. Being labelled or put into a box doesn't acknowledge the way that we are all growing and changing throughout our lives. Who you were at 17 isn't the same person you are at 21, who you were at 23 isn't the same as who you are at 38, and so on. You can be unprepared for driving at one point in your life because you're genuinely not ready for it then. But as you mature, then you can be, as long as you offload unhelpful and out-dated perceptions of yourself first.

I was quite seriously ill when I was a baby and spent a lot of time in and out of hospital. I'm an only child and my parents, especially my mum have always been very protective of me. My mum didn't like the idea of my learning to drive at all, and when Jake and I got together, she even said, 'If you and Jake get married, you won't need to drive, because he can do it' – like we were living a hundred years ago!

I think my parents also see me as someone who 'gives up on things' because I changed my University course and also because I split up with a few eligible boyfriends. But it was only because I knew those relationships wouldn't work for the long term. You're not going to find the right relationship if you're stuck in the wrong one.

My grandmother was keen that I should learn to drive at 17 as she said it gave women safety and independence, and she gifted me money to pay for it. I wasn't mature enough at the time though. I found the lessons very stressful and gave them up.

When I re-started driving lessons in my 20s I could tell my family thought it was just a fad that would fizzle out. Initially I even worried whether they might be right as I wasn't a natural when it came to picking up driving skills and my instructor said it would probably take me significantly more than the average number of lessons. But once I'd truly committed myself I was determined not to keep going until I'd passed my test, no matter how hard it was or how long it took. And I realised that my parents' idea of me as being someone who 'gives up on things' isn't actually true. I've done well in my career, go running in all weathers and have volunteered at a local animal shelter for years, so I've already proved I'm not a flake.

I passed my driving test on the second attempt and went on to take extra training in motorway, night and winter driving. *Millie, 27*

Of course, sometimes it works the other way round, when an able learner exceeds their families expectations.

When it came to learning to drive, everyone thought I'd take longer than my older brother Jay. He's studying to be a lawyer and is a very clever, serious guy. I'm not as good at exams, and I can be lazy and a bit of a joker so my family thought I wouldn't put the work in. But as it turned out, I picked up driving way quicker than Jay. I didn't need as many lessons, and I passed my test first time - he took three attempts. *Ali, 18*

Sometimes people might make remarks and assumptions that are just plain unpleasant and not worth engaging with, though it can be worthwhile to talk your feelings through afterwards with someone who you can rely on to support you.

My school was very sporty and I wasn't. I fitted that cliché of the girl who always got picked last for teams. Anyway, I went to a school reunion and got chatting to a woman who had been in my year. I mentioned I was learning to drive in my 50s and finding it challenging, and she said, 'That doesn't surprise me'. I asked, 'Why's that?' and she replied, "You always were very clumsy'. So rude and patronising! Needless to say I went off to talk to someone else as soon as possible. But her remark hit a nerve as I was feeling very sensitive about learning to drive later in life. I found myself brooding on what she said, and brought it up with my lovely instructor Mark. He said although I was taking longer to learn than an able, younger person I was improving all the time, had a great attitude and he believed I would eventually become a safe and capable driver. That meant a lot and helped me put that woman's spiteful and unhelpful remark behind me. *Jane, 58*

Every life experience is an opportunity to reinvent yourself and how people see you, and that includes learning to drive. As the saying goes, actions speak louder than words, and the best way to overcome any doubters is to take practical actions that are taking you towards the person and the driver that you want to be.

Here are just a few examples – see if you can think of a way you can adapt them to your particular circumstances:

If you're an older driver, find a patient instructor who has experience working with more mature learners

If you've got a particular physical, neurological or mental health condition, ask your doctor or therapist for help in finding an instructor who can tailor their tuition to your particular needs

If people think you're 'lazy' or 'flaky', prove them wrong by always being prepared for your lessons in plenty of time, working hard during them and doing plenty of revision for your Theory Test

6. You're not the only one who cries driving lessons

Have you ever felt upset or tearful during a driving lesson? If so you're not alone – it's far more common than you think.

Practising reversing manoeuvres often had me crying with frustration. Especially when I felt I'd made progress in one lesson, only to have forgotten everything by the next. My instructor was very kind. She'd just smile patiently and say, 'waterworks again, Millie?' *Millie, 27*

I cried in front of my driving instructor, Henry. It was shortly before my driving test and he was, quite rightly, keeping me to a high standard. Anyway, I'd had a tough time for personal reasons earlier that day and when I got into the car and he started to talk about issues that had come up in our previous lesson that we needed to work on, I just started crying. I work as a barrister and normally keep a tight hold of my emotions – even if a case is going badly, I'm trained not to show it. But here I was, sobbing my heart out in front of my instructor. To make matters worse I'm not a dignified crier, the sort where a single tear wells up, trickles down my dewy cheek and that's that. Once I get going I'm the full-on, heaving sobs, bring me a huge box of tissues because I'm going to need all of them, variety. At that point I wanted nothing more than to get out of the car, into my house, crawl under the duvet and abandon myself to a lengthy session of miserable wailing.

I apologised to Henry and said that I would of course pay for the lesson but that I didn't feel up to taking it. To my surprise he urged me to reconsider. He said that in the future there may be times when I would have to drive when upset, such as taking a family member to the hospital in an emergency and it would be good for me to get practice in now when he was here to guide me.

I could see the sense in what he was saying, and managed to calm myself down enough to focus on the lesson. Henry very sensibly kept us to safe, familiar routes (and had one foot hovering over the dual control, I'm sure). We also practised some manoeuvres in a deserted car park. It was an uncomfortable experience, but also a very worthwhile one. *Chloe, 42*

I was close to tears after failing my first driving test. I'd worked so hard, both during my lessons and in the horrible call-centre job I took to pay for them. I'd also really wanted to pass to impress an ex-girlfriend who'd used to tease me about the fact she could drive and I couldn't. It seems so stupid now, but I was only 19 at the time. My driving instructor drove me home and started to chat about the test and what we could do to make the next one a success. But I was so choked up I knew I wouldn't be able to talk without getting tearful, so I just looked out of the window. He took the hint and we drove home in silence. I did have a cry in front of my mum though. She was brilliant and very supportive. We had a nice supper together, I took our dog for a walk and then spent the rest of the evening gaming. By bedtime I felt a lot better. *Nathan, 25*

Even celebrities can be emotionally floored by driving test disappointment. In his autobiography pop star Justin Bieber admitted to crying after failing his written driving theory test. His mum had driven to give him a lift home, but he refused to get in the car with her as he was embarrassed about becoming tearful, and chose to walk home in the rain by himself instead.

Some people are natural, confident drivers who breeze through their lessons and tests without a care in the world. The rest of us find at least some parts of the process stressful – whether that's mastering the driving skills themselves, having to shoehorn time for lessons into our busy lives, acute anxiety about how much the whole process is costing, or a combination of all three.

Add in the fact that we all have good days and bad ones in our everyday life, it's not surprising if sometimes the demands of a driving lesson can be the final straw that has you breaking down in tears. But it's important to realise that crying is a) totally normal and b) totally OK.

Crying during a driving lesson or after a failed test is nothing to be ashamed of. Firstly I'd want to say don't be embarrassed. We driving instructors are used to seeing tears from learners of all ages, and in both men and women. Sometimes it's because they are going through a difficult time in their life and their feelings spill over into their lesson. Other times it's because they're someone who cries easily and it's a good form of release for them. And then, the final reason is that I've unknowingly been pushing them too hard, not realising how overwhelmed they've been feeling. If a pupil reveals they're upset because they are finding the lessons too difficult, then I see that as an opportunity for us to have deeper communication and for me to adjust my teaching style to a pace they feel comfortable with. Ideally though I'd love to make those adjustments earlier, so I'd urge any learner who feels upset during lessons to tell their instructor. Quality instructors want to help, and you can work out a plan together for making lessons less challenging. *Danielle, 56, driving instructor*

Learning to drive is a complex skill and it's not linear either. One week a learner might feel they've finally cracked reverse parking and the following lesson they're back struggling again. This is a natural part of the process as the necessary skills become integrated. But it can also feel frustrating and disheartening, and it's natural that people might become upset. I always tell pupils that as long as they pay attention and are committed to learning they will always be making progress, even at times when it might feel as if they're not. And I also urge them to share their feelings with me. If they have had a difficult day and there are some aspects of driving practice they don't feel up to, that's fine – we can work on something else and return to the more challenging skills another time. *Ravi, 43, driving instructor*

If you do become upset during your driving lessons because of driving-related issues, it's important to communicate what's bothering you to your instructor. If they don't know, they won't be able to help you. If you find a face-to-face discussion too difficult, then send them a text or an online message.

If you're upset for personal reasons, it's up to you how much you tell them. If you've got the sort of relationship where it feels OK to mention that you haven't got the exam results you were hoping for, or that you've had a relationship breakup then do. But if you'd rather keep your private life private just say something along the lines of 'I've had a difficult day because of personal reasons and I'd rather not tackle that busy dual carriageway today. Can we practice manoeuvres instead?'

Once you've got your licence there might be times when you're upset but still feel you have to drive. But do try to avoid or postpone it unless it's a genuine emergency, as studies have shown that you're more likely to become involved in a road accident. For example research by the Transportation Unit in the USA discovered that people who are observably emotionally agitated, crying or angry are ten times more likely to be involved in an crash.

> Shortly after passing my driving test I was at my boyfriend's home in Bristol. Our relationship hadn't been great for a while and we finally agreed to split up. I was due to drive home to Cardiff that afternoon, but felt too shaky to get behind the wheel straight away. So instead I went for a walk in a nearby park, and had a snack and coffee in a cafe. Afterwards I felt stronger and calmer and knew I'd be able to drive home safely. *Rukmini, 33*

7. Pet power

Spending time with your pet can help calm and comfort you when you're feeling stressed about driving. They love you unconditionally and couldn't care less whether you can do a parallel park or not.

> My cat Suky is very sweet and cuddly and spending time with her always used to help calm me down after a difficult driving lesson or yet another failed test. *Kira, 19*

> My family keeps horses at a nearby livery stables. My brother and I went out for a ride the afternoon before my driving test and it helped me stay calm. I passed first time and it was great to know that I could now drive out to ride our horses without having to get a lift from anyone. *Jack, 18*

Also, caring for your pet can be a powerful motivator to getting your driving licence. For example you can take your dog on longer, varied walks and if you need to take your pet to the vet it's much easier with your own transport.

> My only reason for learning to drive was because changes to the bus timetables meant it would take almost two extra hours for me to get home from work and I'd have to leave my rescue dog, Dora alone for too long. I found lessons very hard, but every time I thought of giving them up I'd look

at her loving face and think, 'I'm doing this for you'. *Joanne, 48*

Our cat Jumbo will only be affectionate when he feels like it, so I certainly couldn't rely on him comforting me after a difficult lesson. But my husband and I love him dearly, and when he became ill and needed an operation we were both very worried. I hadn't passed my driving test at that point, so I knew I was going to have to take him to the vet in a taxi. He'd always hated going in his cat carrier and during the drive he yowled all the way and I could tell the taxi driver was very annoyed. When it was time to bring him home I contacted another firm as I was worried the first would refuse to take us again. Luckily Jumbo was still under sedation during that journey, so it was fine.

There are so many things I appreciate about having passed my driving test, but knowing I can take Jumbo to the vet in our own car, whether for a check-up on or in an emergency means so much to me. *Jane, 58*

CHAPTER 5

SUCCESS ON DRIVING TEST DAY

Congratulations! You've made it to driving test day. Your instructor wouldn't have put you in for your test if they didn't know you are capable of passing, so you've already reached test standard and that means you should be very proud of yourself. Now it's a case of keeping your nerves at bay, driving well and showing your examiner what you're capable of.

1. Driving test basics

Get all the essentials you'll need for your driving test prepared the previous day. This will include the necessary paperwork, such as your provisional licence and additional information required by your country or state. These requirements can change over time so check them out on your government website. If you need glasses or contact lenses to drive, make sure they are to hand and if your hair is long then have something to tie it back to ensure the examiner can see your eye movements. Comfortable shoes are essential, and it's best to choose ones that you've driven in many times before. You might like to take along a bottle of water and a snack, and something such as a book to distract you in the driving test waiting room.

2. Bananas and Bach Rescue Remedy

These two items are mentioned in virtually every article you will ever read about passing your driving test, so I make no excuse for flagging them up here.

Bach Rescue Remedy is a combination of flower essences and although it's not in any way scientifically proven it has a reputation among learner drivers for being helpful in stressful situations. It can be taken in drops, or in other forms such as pastilles and is available from health food shops.

Bananas

Bananas are known as the 'driving test superfood'. They are full of B vitamins, tryptophan and potassium, all of which can help lower your anxiety levels. Unless you absolutely hate bananas, I'd strongly advise you to eat one

3. The build-up to your test

If you ask most people when they'd like to take their driving test, most would choose the 'sweet spot' of mid-morning. After the rush hour, but not far enough into the day that you'll have too much time to fret about it.

But of course, most candidates have to take whatever test slot they can get, rather than one they might choose and you could well have a test that's much later in the day. Aim to avoid thinking about your driving test as much as possible, and to focus on work, college or other tasks. If there are any 'difficult conversations' that you might potentially have with any colleagues, tutors, partners or friends then give them a swerve. Even minor matters can escalate unexpectedly and leave you feeling agitated, and that's really not what you want right now.

One of my flatmates is terrible about doing the washing up, but because our work schedules are very different I don't often see her to tackle her about it. On the morning of my second driving test she was around and I was going to say something then but then I thought better of it as she can be quite moody and I didn't want to start this important day with a row. *Kim, 22*

4. Eat something

One of the most common effects of nerves is to make us lose our appetite. But do try to eat breakfast, lunch and supper too, depending on the time of your test. If you can't manage much just have a smaller portion rather than skipping food altogether. It will keep your blood sugar levels more constant, and help your concentration.

5. Use relaxation techniques

Use the relaxation techniques mentioned earlier in this book, such as the 'It can all be easy' visualisation and breathing exercises. You can also use affirmations, either test-specific ones such as 'I am a good, capable driver' or general ones such as 'Everything is going well for me' or 'Today is a great day'. I go into more detail about relaxation techniques in my book *50 Ways to Overcome Driving Test Nerves.*

6. Show unhelpful thoughts the door

It's understandable that just before your driving test you'll be worried about failing and what that might involve – financial consequences, having to face disappointed parents or your instructor and the prospect of more lessons. But the fact is none of these thoughts will help you at this stage of the proceedings so there's no point in allowing them into your head.

> Someone once said to me that your fears are like bullies and gatecrashers. They will barge into your mind and take over if you let them. It's your job to keep them in their place. So when I woke up on the morning of my driving test and all these worries flooded in about money and about how I needed to be able to drive for my new job (I may have told them I already could...), I just thought firmly, NO! I imagined myself closing the door on all these fears like they were unwanted cold callers, firmly saying 'goodbye' or 'not today thank you'. I decided to replace them with more positive thoughts such as, 'I deserve to pass my test' and 'I am ready to drive alone'.
> *Marcelle, 26*

7. Use your driving instructor's car to take your test

It really is best to use your driving instructor's car for your test. Adapting other vehicles for the test can be complicated

– for example, you have to buy additional items such as an extra interior rear-view mirror for the examiner, and also arrange with your insurer to extend your cover for a driving test. Also, being in a dual-controlled car will make the examiner feel more secure.

8. Have a lesson with your instructor beforehand - but don't worry about how it goes

It can be a good idea to have one-hour lesson with your instructor beforehand, just to settle into your driving. But if it's a complete disaster don't worry – you can still go on to have a successful test.

> I made such a mess of my pre-test lesson. I got things wrong that I'd been handling well for weeks. But my instructor Emily just said, 'Don't worry, you've got those mistakes out of your system and now you can go on to pass.' - and I did! *Sasha, 17*

9. Calling Dr Stage!

Actors and performers are very familiar with 'Dr Stage'. This is the phenomenon that for the time they are on stage, any health issues or personal worries they might have are temporarily put on hold, as their attention shifts to totally being in the moment. You may have been in the audience for a fantastic gig where the singer is going through a messy break-up, the guitarist has a splitting headache and the drummer is worried sick about his dog's upcoming operation. But none of it affected the quality of the music or the connection the band shared with the audience because the intense focus on their performance (also known as 'Dr Stage') temporarily lifted the band members beyond their everyday worries and concerns and helped them be their best selves.

You too can call on 'Dr Stage' in that anxious time just before your driving test. You might be worrying over something significant, or you could be fretting about minor matters, such as convincing yourself that you are going down with some unknown malaise, you should have worn a different pair of shoes or whatever. Remind yourself that although you might be feeling anxious and distracted now, when you're at the wheel Dr Stage will have administered his tonic, you'll be driving brilliantly and your driving examiner will become your admiring audience.

> I'm lucky enough to be a very healthy person but just before each of my driving tests I became a complete hypochondriac. I'd be convinced that I had an upset stomach or that sinus problems that hadn't bothered me for years were flaring up again. But the minute I started driving I was miraculously cured. By my final test I could see my 'mystery symptoms' for what they were and ignore them. *Jenny, 37*

10. Impress your examiner

It's OK, you don't have to do anything special to impress your examiner, other than drive as capably as you have with your instructor. They will only be judging you on your driving, and are trained to treat all candidates exactly the same. This can sometimes mean they come across as more formal that your instructor, who you will have become comfortable with over time. You can chat to your examiner or not during your test – just do whatever feels best for you. If possible, try to forget that they are an 'examiner' and imagine that you're driving around a passenger who asks you to show them a few manoeuvres.

There's a chapter about How to impress your examiner in my book *Driving Test Secrets You Need to Know* which goes into more detail about how best to interact with your examiner and what it's important to avoid. One important tip is - don't say anything that could be misconstrued as a 'gift' or 'bribe' or the test will have to be terminated. Obviously you would never offer an examiner cash, but if for example you are a builder avoid mentioning you could offer them a great deal on a new kitchen in case that's misinterpreted as a bribe.

11. Deal calmly with unexpected events and situations on your driving test

Sometimes events you might never have imagined could come at you from left field during your test. Your aim should be to tackle them calmly and safely, just like you will when you're a qualified driver.

On my third test we were driving along a dual carriageway when I saw some expensive-looking cars up ahead, travelling well under the speed limit. I decided to overtake but it was only when I was alongside them that I realised that they were actually part of a funeral procession, being led by a hearse. I honestly didn't know if I'd done the right thing or not. Was it disrespectful to overtake and would it count as a fault? Back at the test centre I learned I'd failed, but it was because of lack of observations at a junction. Afterwards I did some online research and apparently there aren't any official rules on driving around hearses in the Highway Code. However the guidance from funeral directors is to stay behind them if they're in a 30mph or below zone, but that it's OK to overtake on a dual carriageway. *Sian, 26*

I had just finished a reversing manoeuvre, which I felt had gone well when a wasp flew in through the car's open window. It settled in my hair, which is thick and curly. I could feel it moving around. I'm not keen on the idea of being stung by a wasp, but I'm not especially frightened of them either, so it wasn't too difficult to stay calm. My examiner said he thought that if we waited the wasp would fly away. Shortly afterwards it left the car and we were both very relieved. My examiner asked if I would like a moment to compose myself and I said, yes, took three slow, deep breaths and then told him I was ready to drive on. It was my fifth test and my confidence had been badly knocked by previous failures, but right then I felt proud of the way I'd handled a tricky situation. I drove as well as I could and when we got back to the test centre I discovered that I'd finally passed!' *Kira, 19*

Sometimes your driving instructor might be the one to do or say something you're not expecting.

My driving examiner kept calling me Anna instead of Amber, and I didn't know whether or not to correct her. I didn't mind her getting my name wrong as sometimes people do, but part of me was worried that there'd been some sort of admin mix up, I wasn't the candidate she should be examining and even if I didn't make any major faults I wouldn't be able to officially claim my licence because I wasn't the right person. I was too shy to say anything, so I just drove as well as I could and hoped for the best. Thankfully I did pass and was so relieved. I mentioned the mistake about my name to my instructor as he drove me back home afterwards and he said the best thing would have been to just put her right the first time, and that she wouldn't have minded. *Amber, 30*

My examiner got into the car and adjusted the passenger seat. Turns out she must have misjudged it or been laying back too hard as she basically fell backwards as the seat went horizontal. We both laughed and it broke the ice. It made me feel more relaxed and realise that driving examiners are only human too – and I went on to pass. *Fergus, 20*

11. Drive the car

You have just one job during your driving test – and that is to drive the car. Don't give yourself the 'second job' of trying to second-guess what your examiner thinks you should do in every situation you encounter. That's very counter-pro-ductive, as it's likely to make you uncertain and flustered. Believe in yourself and your ability to drive the car safely and capably, just as your instructor has taught you.

> I took eight attempts to pass my test. I was trying to work out why, and I think one of the main reasons was that I was too aware of my examiner and what they might be thinking. We'd come up to a busy junction and I'd be distracted by whether my examiner would judge me either for pulling out too soon or being over hesitant. It felt as though I was overwhelmed with conflicting thoughts at vital moments, and there wasn't enough space left over in my head for me to make clear decisions. It was only when I decided that I had to forget about my examiner as much as possible and make my own decisions that I finally passed! *Sian, 26*

One of the things I always say to my learners in the driving test waiting room is 'You know how to do this. Trust your own judgement'.
Ravi, 44, driving instructor

CHAPTER 6

IF AT FIRST YOU DON'T SUCCEED

Oh dear, you were hoping you weren't going to have to read this chapter weren't you? Everyone wants a first-time pass, and having to return home feeling sad and deflated is a very miserable feeling. But it's OK. It really is OK. Lots of candiates fail their driving test (or tests) and become safe and capable drivers afterwards, and you can too. Here are some strategies to help you achieve just that.

1. Accept and acknowledge your feelings

For most people, failing a driving test is a painful psychological blow that you'll need time to recover from. You might feel sad, angry, worried about the prospect of future lessons and tests, guilty about having let your parents and instructor down and a whole host of other uncomfortable emotions. Rather than trying to smother or dismiss your feelings, just accept that they are there and that they will become easier in time.

> The morning after my failed driving test my alarm was set for 6am so I could get to my stressful call-centre job, which I hated, to earn money for more driving lessons, which I also hated. *Nathan, 25*

The morning after I'd failed my driving test was horrible. My parents had been moaning non-stop about the cost of my lessons and when I went down to break-fast the next day my dad was angry that I'd failed and wouldn't stop talking about how expensive it was going to be to pay for more lessons and another test. I said I'd stop having them then, but my mum said that would be a waste of all the money they'd already spent. The way they went on you'd have thought I'd failed on purpose, but I hadn't. I'd always tried very hard, both in my lessons and during my test. I was so upset. My instructor is good but quite serious and strict, so I didn't feel I could talk to her about how I felt. Luckily we have a counsellor at our school and you can book in to see them if you have any problems. I've got friends who've done that but I never had. I booked an appointment with the counsellor after my failed driving test and when I saw her I explained what had happened and what my parents had said. Then I just sat there and cried and cried. She was very sympathetic and being able to be honest with someone about my feelings helped a lot. *Octavia, 18*

I'd done lots of positive thinking and visual-isations before my first driving test, and I'd really convinced myself it was in the bag. I

was very disappointed when I didn't succeed.
Georgia, 33

2. Don't make any major decisions

All sort of thoughts and feelings could be churning away within you after a failed test. You might be angry and want to appeal your test result (my advice on this is don't – in the UK even if you are successful in appealing your test result you don't get awarded a pass, just a test fee refund). You might be blaming your instructor and think the answer is to get a new one. You could be blaming yourself and think the answer is to give up driving and resign yourself to a lifetime of taking the bus. But don't take action, or even discuss any of this with anyone for at least a day or two after a failed test. You need a bit of time out to let the emotional bruises heal. In doing so you'll calm down, gain a sense of perspective and whatever decisions you may or may not make in future will be better ones.

> I couldn't believe it when I failed my prac-
> tical driving test. I'm dyslexic and needed a
> few attempts to pass my theory test because
> I don't do well under those sort of exam
> conditions. But I woke up on the morning
> of my driving test 100% expecting to pass. I
> could tell some of the learners in the waiting
> room were nervous, but I was cool. I come
> from a farming family and have had a lot of
> experience driving off-road and also doing
> private practice with my dad and grandad.
> My grandad used to be a driver trainer for

the police. He said he thought I was good, and he's not a guy who gives out compliments easily. So when my examiner told me I'd failed because I'd moved out too quickly at a junction I was too shocked to say anything at the time, but later when my instructor Gavin was driving me home, I got angry. I remembered that junction perfectly and felt there had been plenty of space for me to move out safely! I told Gavin I'd been treated unfairly and that I wanted to appeal. That was on the Friday, and he said he didn't think that was a good idea and gave his reasons and asked me to wait over the weekend and we could discuss it then if I still wanted to. I spent a busy couple of days helping out on the farm, and by Monday I'd calmed down and was ready to take more lessons. Gavin pointed out that I can be over-confident, and that's something I needed to change so I could reach test standard and be a safe driver. So we did a lot more work around improving my judgement at junctions. Then I missed my next test because a traffic accident meant I didn't get to the test centre in time – but I still had to pay for it. I passed the third one without any minors at all, which I was very proud of. *Fergus, 20*

3. Look for the positives

Yes, you did fail your driving test, but if you only made one or two major faults then although you got things wrong, there was also a lot that you got right. Also, having got your first driving test out of the way the next won't feel so daunting.

It's a good idea to write down what you can remember about your test. The route you took, the reasons your examiner gave for failing you, and any other feedback they offered. Also record what you can remember about your feelings – were you nervous all the way through your test, or were there sections where you felt more confident? This will all be useful information to return to and discuss with your instructor in the future.

I felt fine the morning after my failed test. I only had one major fault, and three minor ones. The major was for stopping over the stop line on a zebra crossing, which is something I would never have normally done and was completely out of character. It was just nerves, because I'd let myself get so stressed about the test itself. No matter how my instructor Ravi tried to calm me down, I couldn't stop building it up in my mind into this terrible ordeal. I had these crazy recurring anxiety dreams where I crashed the car, and then all the driving test examiners ganged up on me and chased me from the test centre, brandishing their clipboards. Turns out it the reality of a driving test was rather less eventful. It was just like one of the mock tests Ravi and I had done, except with a different guy in the passenger seat. My examiner was a bit quiet and reserved, but not scary at all. He didn't ask anything of me that I hadn't done many times before. So when he told me during the debrief that there had just been the one major fault, my main feeling was one of relief. I'd completed a driving test and come out the other side in one piece. I had some extra lessons with Ravi between tests and we talked about how important it is to have your driving skills at a level where you can drive capably regardless of your emotional state. With that first test behind me I started to believe in myself as a driver and enjoyed my lessons more than I ever had before. I went into my second test feeling sure I'd pass – and I did! *Maura, 25*

4. Get emotional support – and be kind to yourself

Regardless of your driving test result, the fact remains that you worked hard and did your best. You deserve acknowledgement and praise for that, for being brave enough to try. Now it's time to kick back and give yourself a treat. Take time to do something enjoyable. Maybe lunch with a close friend or your mum, a long dog walk, playing sport, a computer game or trying out a new recipe. Even if you're busy with work or college immediately after your test, consciously choose to take a break when you can, and do something that will soothe and distract you, such as reading a few chapters of a book or watching some fun videos. Treating yourself well rather than beating yourself up over something that now can't be changed is an excellent way to restore your sense of optimism and self-belief.

It took me five attempts to pass my driving test. Each one was worse than the last, as I'd be so hopeful, and then my hopes would be dashed. I knew I was capable, it was just that I seemed to make silly mistakes and self-sabotage when it came to my test, and I didn't understand why. Luckily my family and instructor Emily were great and very supportive, and so was my cat Suky who always comes and cuddles with me when she knows I'm down. *Kira, 19*

My older brother and I are close, and we spoke on the phone after my failed driving test and he could tell how upset I was. He lives in London but said he'd come down for the weekend soon and he'd take me to do something fun, like go paddle-boarding. *Octavia, 18*

I treated myself to a brand new book by my favourite sci-fi author after my first failed driving test. Normally I'd wait until it had reduced in price, but I really needed cheering up. It did help me feel better. *Kim, 22*

5. It's (mostly) best to continue with your lessons

Sometimes learners are so disheartened by failure that they abandon their lessons. But taking time off means that your skills will decline and it will take more time and cost more money for you to pass your test. However, if you're under a lot of emotional stress, or the financial burden is too much then you might have to pause them – this is a situation in which you have to use your own judgement.

6. Work on improving your driving

On your next lesson you and your driving instructor can go over what went wrong during your test and how you can raise your skills so that you'll be successful in your next test – regardless of your emotional state, or road or traffic conditions on the day.

7. Overcoming repeated failures

If you fail your test repeatedly, you might want to look at whether you're being put in for it too soon. Having a lesson with another instructor and asking for honest feedback will help you work out if this is the case. If nerves and anxiety are the root problem, then one strategy is for your driving instructor to get your skills up beyond the level of the regular test – then even if you are a bit below par on the day, you'll still pass. Or if it is anxiety, perhaps it'll just evaporate. People who have experienced multiple failures sometimes experience it like some mysterious shift that comes from no-where.

> I passed my driving test on my eighth attempt. I was driving along and chatting with my examiner and suddenly it dawned on me that I was doing fine. I remember thinking, 'Why have I been making such

a big deal out of this?' I passed and have driven safely in the UK and abroad ever since. *Sian, 26*

8. Believe in yourself

With hard work and persistence, you can pass your test and look forward to a future of happy motoring. Better luck next time!

With all best wishes

Maria xxx

A NOTE FROM THE AUTHOR

Thank you for reading *Driving Test Confidence*. I do hope you enjoyed my book and found it useful.

I'm planning future books in the *Driving Test Confidence* series so do get in touch at maria@mariamccarthy.co.uk if you have any suggestions or feedback, and I'd love to hear about your own driving test pass. You can also find out more at www.mariamccarthy.co.uk and www.drivingtestsecrets.com

Also, if you have time, I'd be ever so grateful for an honest review, even if it's just a few words. Reviews are hugely helpful to authors and will also help other learner drivers find my books.

For even more advice and support to help you pass your driving test do check out my other books:

Driving Test Secrets You Need to Know
50 Ways to Overcome Driving Test Nerves
You can Pass Your Driving Test

For more driving test tips and videos follow me on social media.
twitter/mariamccarthy11
tiktok/drivingtestsecrets
facebook/drivingtestsecrets
instagram/drivingtestsecrets

Printed in Great Britain
by Amazon